DIVALI

A WORLD OF FESTIVALS

DIVALI

Dilip Kadodwala

Evans

Evans Brothers Limited

Published by Evans Brothers Limited
2A Portman Mansions
Chiltern Street
London W1U 6NR
Reprinted 2001, 2002

© copyright Evans Brothers Limited 1998
First published 1998
First published in paperback 1999

British Library Cataloguing in Publication data.

Kadodwala, Dilip
    Divali. – (A world of festivals)
    1. Divali – Juvenile literature
    I. Title
    394.2 65 45

ISBN 0 237 52066 4

Printed in Spain by G.Z. Printek

ACKNOWLEDGEMENTS

Editor: Su Swallow
Design: Raynor Design
Production: Jenny Mulvanny

The Author and Publishers would like to thank
Hema Acharya for her help with this book.

The Author and Publishers would like to thank the
following for permission to reproduce photographs:

Cover Zefa Pictures
Title page Edward Parker/Hutchison Library

page 6 (top right) Trip/P Rauter (bottom left) Edward
Parker/Hutchison Library **page 7** (top) Ann and
Bury Peerless (bottom) Trip/Dinodia **page 8** (left)
Trip/Dinodia (right) Goycoolea/Hutchison Library
page 9 (top) National Museum of India, New Delhi,
Bridgeman Art Library (bottom left) Trip/H Rogers
(bottom right) Trip/H Rogers **page 10** (top) Trip/H
Rogers (bottom) Bipinchandra J. Mistry **page 11**
Trip/H Rogers **page 12** Trip/S Austin **page 13**
Bipinchandra J Mistry **page 14** (top right)
Bipinchandra J Mistry (bottom left) Ann and Bury
Peerless **page 15** (top) Ann and Bury Peerless
(bottom) Trip/H Rogers **page 16** (top) Trip/H
Rogers (bottom) Bipinchandra J Mistry **page 17**
Trip/H Rogers **page 18** (left) Trip/H Rogers (right)
Anthony Cassidy/Tony Stone **page 19** Trip/H
Rogers **page 20 and page 21** Ann and Bury Peerless
page 22 (left) JHC Wilson/Robert Harding Picture
Library (right) Ann and Bury Peerless **page 23** (top)
JHC Wilson/Robert Harding Picture Library
(bottom) Ann and Bury Peerless **page 24** (top)
Trip/Dinodia (bottom) National Museum of India,
New Delhi/Bridgeman Art Library **page 25** (top)
National Museum of India, New Delhi/Bridgeman
Art Library (bottom left) Private Collection/
Bridgeman Art Library (bottom right) Ann and Bury
Peerless **page 26** (top) Image Bank (bottom) Trip/T
Bognar **page 27** (top) Trip/P Rauter (bottom) Ken
Gillham/Robert Harding Picture Library **page 28
and 29** Anthony King/Medimage

Contents

DIVALI AND HINDUISM   6

DIVALI TIME   8

THE FIRST DAY OF DIVALI   10

THE SECOND DAY OF DIVALI   12

THE THIRD DAY OF DIVALI   14

THE LAST DAY OF THE YEAR   16

THE FOURTH DAY OF DIVALI   18

FOOD AND FEASTING   20

THE STORY OF PRINCE RAMA AND SITA   22

RAMA RETURNS   24

FESTIVAL FUN   26

LET'S CELEBRATE!   28

GLOSSARY   30

INDEX   30

Divali and Hinduism

IVALI IS A HINDU FESTIVAL celebrated by Hindus wherever they live in the world. (Sikhs also celebrate Divali but for different reasons.) Most Hindus live in India and Nepal.

Hinduism is one of the world's oldest religions and of all the world's main religions, Hinduism has the third largest number of followers.

Floating oil lamps on a lake in India to celebrate Divali

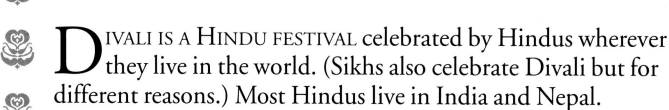

This ornate fan shows Rama, one of the forms of God (see page 22).

ONE GOD

Hindus believe that there is one God, one Supreme Being, called Brahman. Hindus also believe that Brahman can be pictured and thought about in many different forms. This shows the power and presence of God, who is believed to be everywhere. This is why Hindus worship Brahman through many gods and goddesses. The festival of Divali has exciting stories about some of these gods and goddesses.

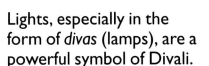

THE MEANING OF DIVALI

The name Divali comes from the word *Deepavali*, which means 'row of lights'. Divali is the most widely celebrated festival in India, although the celebrations differ from place to place.

Hindus in India follow a street procession during Divali.

Lights, especially in the form of *divas* (lamps), are a powerful symbol of Divali.

But there are some things about the festival that are common across the world. The lighting of lamps, called *divas*; cleaning, and sometimes, painting homes; feasting with families and friends; and illuminating homes, shops, streets and public buildings with bright lights – these are some of the ways Divali is celebrated by Hindus wherever they live in the world. The festival can last up to five days.

The most important meaning of the festival is the celebration of the triumph of good over evil. It is also a time for renewing hopes for happiness and prosperity in life.

Divali time

DIVALI OCCURS DURING THE 'DARK HALF' FORTNIGHT OF ASHVIN, which falls in October or November. Bright lights, festive fun and a sense of joy and happiness, in many ways help to brighten the darkness of the autumn month.

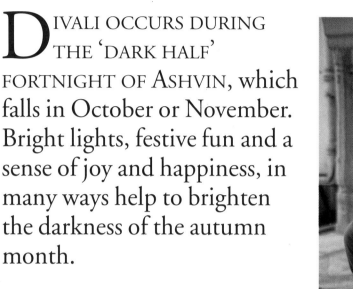

Street lights go up all over India at Divali time.

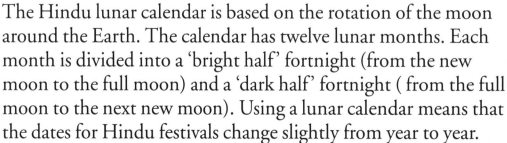

A family gathering round a tray of festival lights

ON THE DARK SIDE

The Hindu lunar calendar is based on the rotation of the moon around the Earth. The calendar has twelve lunar months. Each month is divided into a 'bright half' fortnight (from the new moon to the full moon) and a 'dark half' fortnight (from the full moon to the next new moon). Using a lunar calendar means that the dates for Hindu festivals change slightly from year to year.

Gods and goddesses

Many Hindu festivals are linked to stories of gods and goddesses. Hindus believe that the god Vishnu preserves and protects the world with his goodness. Whenever the power of evil increases in the world, Hindus believe that Vishnu comes down to Earth in a different form to challenge and defeat evil. These forms are called *avataras*. Krishna and Rama are popular *avataras* of Vishnu. Gods are accompanied by goddesses, who are sometimes called *shakti*, meaning energy or power.

Without this energy, gods would be powerless! Divali celebrations are especially a time for telling stories about Vishnu and his wife Lakshmi, and about Krishna, Rama and his wife Sita.

Part of an ancient statue of Vishnu, carved out of red sandstone

Children worshipping at a shrine in a *mandir* (temple). Many Hindus visit a *mandir* during Divali.

Another picture of Vishnu, with some of his *avataras*.

The first day of Divali

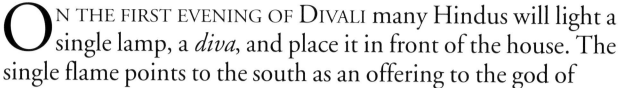

ON THE FIRST EVENING OF DIVALI many Hindus will light a single lamp, a *diva*, and place it in front of the house. The single flame points to the south as an offering to the god of death who is called Yama. It is also a reminder to Hindus that death is a part of life.

▶ The flame of a single *diva* burns in a brass bowl.

SHOWING RESPECT

On this first day of Divali, which Hindus call *Dhana-Trayodashi*, an image or statue of Lakshmi is carefully washed in milk. Hindus use the word *murti* to describe images or figures of gods and goddesses. *Murtis* are treated with great respect and reverence. They are used as part of daily worship, helping worshippers to concentrate on God. Hindus have special shrines in their homes where pictures and

A Hindu woman worships God with *diva* lights, at the family shrine in her home in Britain.

murtis of gods and goddesses are 'housed'. Usually, *murtis* are washed daily, draped with fine clothes and garlands of flowers and treated like kings and queens. It is a popular way for Hindus to show respect and love for the majesty of God.

LAKSHMI AND THE LOTUS FLOWER

Whenever Vishnu comes down to Earth, Lakshmi takes form as his wife. She represents Vishnu's divine energy and power. In one story, it is said that Lakshmi came to Earth standing on a lotus flower. She was created from the churning of an ocean of milk. This is a way of saying that Lakshmi stands for purity, just as the beauty of a lotus flower floating on water is not spoilt by the muddy soil from which it grows. The washing of a *murti* of Lakshmi on the first day of Divali acts as a reminder to Hindus to aim for pure thoughts and deeds in their lives.

This first day is also a time for eating sweets made from thickened milk – a treat reapeated throughout the time of Divali festivities!

The goddess Lakshmi, standing on a lotus flower. Can you see other lotus flowers in the picture?

11

The second day of Divali

T HE SECOND DAY OF DIVALI is called *Narak Chaturdashi.* This day celebrates the victory of the god Krishna over the demon Narakasur.

FEASTING AND FIREWORKS

This is a day when Hindus arise earlier than usual. The men, especially, will rub their bodies with perfumed oils before bathing. Afterwards, clean clothes are worn; some people wear new ones. A large breakfast is enjoyed, people eating with relatives and friends. In the morning and in the evening, a mix of bright and loud fireworks are set off in an atmosphere of joyful fun and noise. Special sweet dishes are served as part of the midday meal. Houses are lit with oil lamps in the evening. In some parts of India, houses with flat roofs are also brightly lit with rows of *divas.* This creates an enchanting, magical atmosphere!

Fireworks help to make Divali an exciting festival!

THE DEFEAT OF NARAKASUR

There are different versions of the story of Narakasur and his defeat by Krishna. In one popular version, Narakasur is shown as a demon of filth, covered in dirt. He was a giant who was often good but who, at times, behaved very badly. He used to kidnap beautiful young women and force them to live with him. It is said that this misfortune fell on some 16,000 women. Eventually, their cries for rescue were heard by Vishnu, who came in the form of Krishna.

First, Krishna had to fight with a five-headed monster who guarded the demon's home. Then,

before the demon Narakasur was destroyed, Krishna granted him one last request, because of the good deeds he had done. Narakasur hoped that his death might bring joy to others. So, before being killed, he cried "Let this day be celebrated as a day of feasting in the world!" His request was granted by Krishna and the women were freed. For Hindus, this story is a reminder that good can still come out of evil.

A dish of tantalising food for Divali – with vegetable curry, rice, *puri* (a form of Indian bread) and a choice of sweets

The third day of Divali

T HE THIRD DAY OF DIVALI is called *Lakshmi Pujan*. On this day and night the goddess Lakshmi is worshipped in many parts of the Hindu world.

PURITY AND PERFECTION

Lakshmi represents good fortune, wealth and beauty. Hindus invite the goddess to enter their homes and bless them with good health, happiness and good fortune. *Divas* are lit to welcome the goddess into the homes and lives of the worshippers. Even poor people who cannot afford the oil to light too many *divas* will make sure that at least a single *diva* is lit so that Lakshmi may bless them.

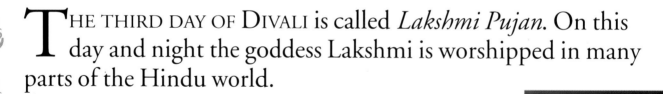

Pictures of Lakshmi show her either standing or sitting on a lotus flower. She has four hands. This is a way of showing her different qualities and powers. In two of her hands, she carries lotus flowers, which are signs of purity and perfection. The third hand with an upraised palm is a sign of Lakshmi offering her worshippers protection from evil. From her fourth hand gold coins fall. This is a sign of Lakshmi's power to bring riches and prosperity to those who worship her with purity and unselfishness in their hearts.

A *diva* lamp decorated with a peacock's tail. Several animals are linked to Hindu gods and goddesses.

A traditional picture of Lakshmi, sitting on a lotus flower

A SIGN OF WELCOME

Another way of welcoming the goddess Lakshmi into people's homes is by drawing *rangoli* patterns on the floor of the entrance of each house. A *rangoli* is a sign of welcome. Some Hindus draw one daily as a way of welcoming guests. The patterns are

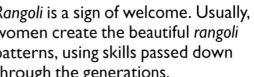

Rangoli is a sign of welcome. Usually, women create the beautiful *rangoli* patterns, using skills passed down through the generations.

made with fingers using flour, rice grains or coloured chalk. The shape of the pattern can be a square, rectangle or a circle. Sometimes, they can be a mix of all three shapes and may also have drawings of lotus flowers, like the borders in this book, or other, geometric designs.

In the West, some Hindu communities have competitions for children to design *rangoli* patterns and prizes are given for the best designs during Divali celebrations.

This *rangoli* pattern uses the *swastika*, a sign of 'wellbeing'.

The last day of the year

O N THE LAST DAY OF THE OLD YEAR, which is the third day of Divali, houses are cleaned from top to bottom. It is a bit like spring cleaning! It is believed that clean homes are blessed by Lakshmi. Some Hindus will also redecorate their homes.

These days, many Hindus around the world exchange greetings cards at Divali. The cards often have pictures of gods and goddesses.

DIVALI DECORATIONS

Apart from a *rangoli* pattern at the entrance of a home, the front door is decorated with a garland or piece of cloth called a *toran*. A *toran* is made of flower petals and betel nut leaves, which are strung together and hung at the top of the front door. If a *toran* is made from cloth, it has rich patterns which may include elephants, peacocks and the symbol *aum*. *Aum* is a sacred Hindu sign and syllable for God. Hindus say this syllable at the start and end of their prayers and worship.

This *toran* is made from cotton. It is hung over the entrance of a home.

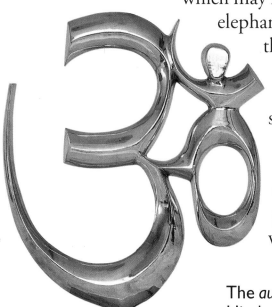

The *aum* – the sacred Hindu syllable representing the sound of God

COINS AND ACCOUNTS

For Hindus who are in business and trade, this day is marked by the settling of accounts. This is another reason why the goddess Lakshmi is so important during this festival. She is worshipped in the hope that in the new 'financial' year of trading, she will bring prosperity. A special ceremony called *Lakshmi Pujan* is done either in the home shrine or at a Hindu temple (*mandir*). The ceremony is done firstly by washing a gold or silver coin in a liquid. The liquid is made by mixing water, milk, yoghurt, and a little sugar and butter. Then the coin is marked with a dot of *kum kum*. This is a red or saffron-coloured powder which is made into a paste. After this, the coin is placed in an account book and a string is tied

For Hindus in business, Divali marks a time for the settling of accounts. A special ceremony called *Lakshmi Pujan* is performed.

around the book. Sometimes, Hindus put a small picture of Lakshmi on the coin before it is put into the book. Prayers are recited, in the hope that the new year will bring good fortune. The account book is then left overnight in the family shrine at home, surrounded by the *murtis* of gods and goddesses.

The fourth day of Divali

THE FOURTH DAY OF DIVALI is the first day of the month of Kartik. It is a day filled with hope and promise of good things. For traders, it is the start of a new financial year. For other Hindus, new ventures are also started on this joyous new year's day.

PRESENTS AND PARTIES

Wherever possible, new clothes are worn on this day. A married woman will receive a present from her husband, usually a gold ornament. Family members also give and receive presents. Any quarrels between friends and relatives are forgotten. People greet each other by saying, *'Sal Mubarak'*, which means 'Happy New Year!' It is a day for visiting friends and relatives and exchanging gifts of food, usually a tantalising, mouth-watering choice of

Shopping for saris in western India

Mother and daughter celebrate Divali by wearing bright new clothes.

For children, especially, Divali is a glittering and joyous time. It is also a time for sharing.

sweets, made of all shapes and sizes. Children and adults alike share in the feasting!

VISITING A TEMPLE

Hindus are not usually expected to visit a *mandir* – a temple – every day. Mostly, Hindus worship at home. But on this day of Divali many Hindu families go to the *mandir*. It is a special occasion for worshippers to gather together and share in the celebrations.

The sharing of food is also an important part of the celebrations. People take offerings of sweetmeats to the *mandir*. This food is called *ankoot*, which means 'mountain of food'. The food is offered to the gods and goddesses in the *mandir* in the shape of a mountain. After a special ceremony, the food is shared out among the worshippers.

FIREWORKS AND LIGHT

As darkness falls, *divas* are lit and illuminations go up everywhere. The loud blast of fireworks fills the air, mingling with the noise of happy people out in the streets celebrating the new year. The sound of music and laughter continues well into the night!

SISTER'S DAY

The fifth day of Divali is celebrated as Sister's Day. Married men do not eat any food cooked by their wives. Instead, they visit their sister's house, where they are treated to a delicious meal.

Of course, many Hindu men have more than one sister and sisters may have more than one brother! In this case, each sister will take her turn over the years to welcome their brothers. Unless the brother feels that he can eat more than one big meal in a day!

19

Food and feasting

DIVALI IS A TIME FOR EATING SPECIAL FOOD. But more than that it is a time for being thankful for what the earth offers in the form of food. It is also a time for sharing and showing generosity. These teachings are put across to Hindu children through two stories.

Drying rice grains in southern India. Divali is a time for being thankful for plentiful harvests.

KRISHNA AND THE MOUNTAIN

In the village of Gokula, many years ago, the people prayed to the god Indra. They believed that Indra sent the rains which made their crops grow. But Krishna came along and persuaded the people to worship the mountain Govardhan, because the mountain and the land around it were fertile. The cows grazed on the rich grass and in turn gave plentiful milk and butter to the villagers. This did not please Indra. One night, as the villagers slept, Indra sought revenge. He sent thunder and torrential rain down on the village. The people cried to Krishna for help. Krishna saved the villagers by lifting the top of the mountain with his finger. Underneath it, the people gathered until the storm passed away.

Krishna lifts the mountain and saves the villagers from drowning.

The offering of food to God on this day of Divali is a reminder to Hindus of the importance of food and it is a time for being thankful to God for the bounty of nature. The sharing of food with others also helps to strengthen the bond of friendship and community between Hindus.

KING BALI AND THE DWARF

The other story concerns King Bali, who was a generous ruler. But he was also very ambitious. Some of the gods pleaded with Vishnu to check King Bali's power. Vishnu came to Earth in the form of a dwarf dressed as a priest. The dwarf approached King Bali and said, "You are the ruler of the three worlds: the Earth, the world above the skies and the underworld. Would you give me the space that I could cover with three strides?" King Bali laughed. Surely a dwarf could not cover much ground, thought the King, who agreed to the dwarf's request. At this point, the dwarf changed into Vishnu and his three strides covered the earth, the skies and the whole universe! King Bali was sent to the underworld.

As part of the Divali celebrations, some Hindus remember King Bali. In Bombay, for example, shapes of King Bali are made out of cooked flour or rice flour and placed on a silver tray. A prayer is said: 'May Bali's empire be restored and all evil disappear.'

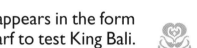

Vishnu appears in the form of a dwarf to test King Bali.

The story of Prince Rama and Sita

IN NORTHERN INDIA DIVALI CELEBRATES the return of Prince Rama to the kingdom of Ayodhya. Hindus think of Rama as one of the incarnations of the god Vishnu. The story of Rama is told in a long poem called the *Ramayana*.

Ramayana was written over two thousand years ago. The story is acted out all over India over a period of a month. These plays are called the *Rama Lila*. The drama reaches a climax when Rama defeats an evil demon. One of the main messages of the *Ramayana* is that the power of goodness overcomes evil.

Crowds gather to watch a perfomance of *Rama Lila*.

A huge model of an evil demon is burned as a way of showing the triumph of good over evil.

A QUEEN'S WISH

Rama was a great warrior king. His adventures start when he is sent off to a forest for fourteen years. Rama was the eldest son of King Dasharatha. The King had three wives and they all lived in the royal city of Ayodhya. Once, a long time ago, one of the King's wives, called Queen Kaikeyi, had saved his life when he was in grave danger. So the King granted Kaikeyi two wishes. When the time came for Rama to be crowned as king, Kaikeyi was jealous. She wanted her son, Prince Bharat, to be the ruler instead. So she went to King Dasharatha and reminded him that he would grant her two wishes. She said that she wanted Bharat to be king and that Rama and his wife Sita should be sent away to the forest for fourteen years.

An actress dressed up to act the part of the beautiful Sita

OFF TO THE FOREST

The old king was very sad but he kept his promise about the two wishes. Rama was a dutiful son who loved and obeyed his father. He agreed to be banished

to the forest. Sita was a dutiful wife to Rama. She could not bear to be parted from her husband so she insisted that she should go with Rama. They were also joined by Rama's stepbrother called Lakshman. When Bharat saw that Rama had been cheated out of being king, he placed Rama's sandals on the throne. This was to show that Bharat would only rule the kingdom until Rama returned from the forest.

How does the story end? Turn over the page and find out!

Rama seated with his beautiful wife Sita. Rama's stepbrother is standing behind them.

Rama returns

LIFE IN THE FOREST WAS HARD for Rama, Sita and Lakshman. There were wild animals and demons in the forest. The king of the demons was called Ravana.

RAVANA SEEKS REVENGE

One day, Ravana's sister saw Rama. She wanted to marry him but Rama said that he was already married. This made her very angry and she tried to kill Sita. As a punishment, Lakshman cut off her nose and ears. So Ravana sought revenge. He asked his uncle, who was a magician, to change himself into a golden deer. When Sita saw the deer, she wanted to keep it. So she sent Rama after the deer. When Rama did not return, Sita asked Lakshman to find him. Before he left, Lakshman drew a magic circle of protection and asked Sita to stay inside it.

A giant wooden model of Ravana, the many-headed king of the demons

Lakshman fires an arrow at Ravana's sister.

SITA IS CAPTURED

While Lakshman was away finding Rama, the demon Ravana disguised himself as a hermit begging for food. When Sita saw him she stepped out of the magic circle to give him some food. As soon as she stepped out, Ravana grabbed her and took her away to his island kingdom of Lanka. Ravana tried to persuade Sita to marry him. But she refused. Ravana imprisoned her, hoping she might change her mind.

SITA IS RESCUED

It was not too long before Rama and Lakshman realised that they had been tricked. They began searching for Sita but they could not find her anywhere. Then a bird called Jatayu told them what had happened to Sita. Rama asked the king of the monkeys, Hanuman, for help. Hanuman gathered an army and they set off to find Sita. They built a bridge of stones to cross over to the island where Ravana held Sita captive. After a long battle, Sita was rescued. Rama defeated the ten-headed demon Ravana by using a special bow and arrow.

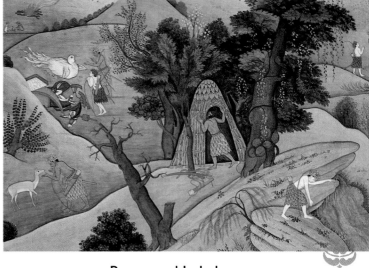

Rama and Lakshma wandering in search of Sita.

For Hindus, Hanuman stands for strength and energy. They try to follow Hanuman's example of devotion to Rama.

A battle scene from the *Ramayana*, after which Sita was finally rescued

RETURN TO AYODHYA

The fourteen years of exile in the forest came to an end. The day Rama, Sita and Lakshman returned to Ayodhya, the people welcomed them back by lighting rows of clay lamps. Great celebrations were held and everyone was happy for Rama to be the king! For Hindus today, the story of Rama's victory over Ravana is a celebration of the victory of good over evil.

Festival fun!

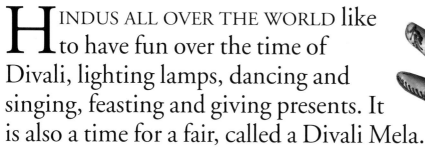

HINDUS ALL OVER THE WORLD like to have fun over the time of Divali, lighting lamps, dancing and singing, feasting and giving presents. It is also a time for a fair, called a Divali Mela.

JOINING TOGETHER

Many of the joyous *melas* in India are to be found in the towns and villages. *Mela* means to meet up, to gather together. In the countryside, a *mela* also becomes a market day when farmers buy and sell farm produce. In the towns, traders take the chance to sell brightly coloured clothes and shiny glass bangles. The bangles are especially attractive to girls and women who pick them out to match their new Divali clothes. Another attraction for girls and women are stalls where they can have beautiful *henna* designs painted on their

A hand richly decorated with henna

hands. Henna is a brown dye made from a plant. The rich designs add to the beautiful clothes and jewellery worn by the female revellers. Food stalls are also found everywhere, selling sweet and spicy snacks and a variety of fruity and fizzy drinks to ready customers!

Festive clothes and ornaments fit for a great festival!

THE FUN OF THE FAIR

Amid the noise and bustle of the crowds, *mela* entertainers add to the festive fun. Jugglers and acrobats perform feats which leave the crowds spellbound! Snake charmers and fortune tellers also provide festive fun. Children delight in having a go on big ferris wheels and having rides on elephants and camels. Puppet shows are another attraction for children and adults alike. As darkness falls, huge firework displays cover the night skies. Tiredness does not stop the festive fun from continuing well into the night!

CELEBRATIONS IN THE WEST

Divali is not a public holiday in the West, as it is in India and Nepal. But this does not stop Hindus from celebrating, especially if the festival falls over a week-end. In large cities in Britain, such as London and Leicester, colourful lights and decorations on

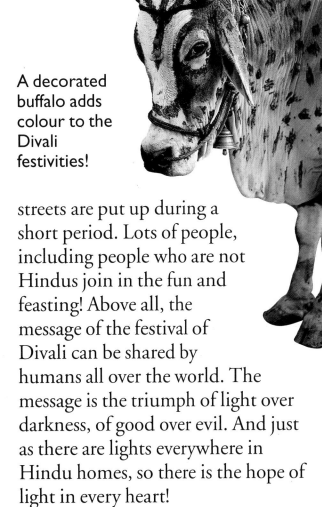

A decorated buffalo adds colour to the Divali festivities!

streets are put up during a short period. Lots of people, including people who are not Hindus join in the fun and feasting! Above all, the message of the festival of Divali can be shared by humans all over the world. The message is the triumph of light over darkness, of good over evil. And just as there are lights everywhere in Hindu homes, so there is the hope of light in every heart!

A splash of city lights offer greetings to one and all. Divali is celebrated by Hindus all over the world. This picture was taken in Singapore.

 Let's celebrate!

JOIN IN THE FUN OF DIVALI! Try making this mask (read about Hanuman on page 25) and create your own signs of welcome with these rangoli patterns (see page 15).

MAKING A HANUMAN MASK

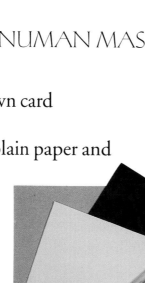

You will need:
1 a sheet of thick brown card
2 gold or yellow card
3 coloured paper, or plain paper and paints or crayons
4 a black marker pen
5 safe scissors
6 PVA glue
7 a long stick
8 sticky tape

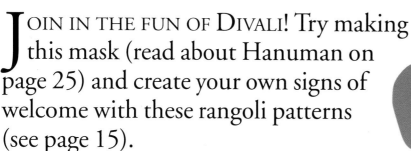

All you have to do is:

1 Cut out the mask's shape using the picture to help you. Remember to make it big enough to cover your face.

2 Cut out Hanuman's face from the coloured paper and stick it on the head. Draw in the nose and the mouth.

3 Draw in the eyes and make small holes in the centre of them.

4 Cut out a crown and other decorations and stick them on the mask.

5 Tape the stick on to the back of the mask with sticky tape. Now your mask is ready.

MAKING RANGOLI PATTERNS

You will need:
1 plain white paper
2 black paper
3 a black marker pen and coloured markers or paints
4 safe scissors
5 PVA glue

All you need to do is:
1 Copy the *rangoli* patterns in the picture on to white paper. You can leave them in black and white or you could colour them in.
2 Cut out the patterns and stick them on to black paper.
3 Look for other *rangoli* patterns in this book and copy the one you like best.

29

Glossary

aum   (sometimes spelt *om*) a sacred Hindu word and sign for God

avatar   God who comes down to Earth in different forms, for example, as Rama and Krishna, to destroy evil

diva   a lamp light made out of twisted cotton wool which is dipped in melted butter

mandir   a Hindu place of worship, sometimes called a temple

mela   a fair

murti   an image or figure of a god or a goddess

Ramayana   a sacred Hindu scripture in the form of a poem of 24,000 verses arranged in seven books

Rama Lila   a series of plays based on stories from the *Ramayana*

Index

Brahman   6
Britain   27

calendar   8
coins   14, 17

diva   7, 10, 12, 14, 19

food   13, 18, 19, 20, 21, 24, 26

Hanuman   25

India   6, 26, 27

King Bali   21
King Dasharatha   23
Krishna   9, 12, 13, 20

Lakshmi   9, 11, 14, 15, 16, 17
Lakshmi Pujan   14, 17
lotus flowers   11, 14, 15

mandir   9, 17, 19

murti   10, 11

Rama   9, 22, 23, 24, 25
Rama Lila   22
Ramayana   22
rangoli   15, 16
Ravana   24, 25

Sita   9, 23, 24, 25

Vishnu   9, 11, 13, 21, 22